A SEASON OF TRAGEDY

Connie Capps

ISBN 979-8-89428-297-8 (paperback)
ISBN 979-8-89428-298-5 (digital)

Copyright © 2024 by Connie Capps

All rights reserved. No part of this publication may be reproduced, distributed, or transmitted in any form or by any means, including photocopying, recording, or other electronic or mechanical methods without the prior written permission of the publisher. For permission requests, solicit the publisher via the address below.

Christian Faith Publishing
832 Park Avenue
Meadville, PA 16335
www.christianfaithpublishing.com

Printed in the United States of America

To the most precious gifts I have ever received, my two wonderful sons, Aaron and Nicholas. You are missed daily, and I love you more than you know or will ever know. I cannot wait to see you again when God calls me home.

Before publication of this book, my brother James was killed in a motorcycle accident in February 2024. I would also like to dedicate this book in his honor. James knew I had written this book but had not had it published yet.

James and I were very close at the time of his passing. However, that always was not the case. During my season of tragedy our brother-sister relationship changed. God answered my prayers and for the first time in years we were close.

Preface

This book is my true testimony of events that happened during my season of tragedy. This book would not have been possible without the help of the Lord, Yvon Damon, and my brother James Edward Bolt Jr.

Introduction

A lot of people have had some kind of tragedy in their lives at one time or another, but three deaths within two years, and my whole family is gone.

> There is a time, *and a season for every activity under the heavens*, a time to be born and a time to die, a time plant and a time to uproot, a time to kill and a time to heal, a time to tear down and a time to build, a time to weep and a time to laugh, a time to mourn and a time to dance, a time to scatter and a time to gather them, a time to embrace and a time to refrain from embracing, a time to search and

a time to give up, a time to keep and a time to throw away, a time to tear and a time to mend, a time to be silent and a time to speak, a time to love and a time to hate, a time for war and a time for peace. (Ecclesiastes 3:1–5, emphasis added)

Contents

Preface v

Introduction vii

Chapter 1: Married to a Monster 1

Chapter 2: The Beginning of the End............. 10

Chapter 3: Life after the Monster 19

Chapter 4: Tragedy.. 28

Chapter 5: The Funeral 34

Chapter 6: Not Again, God, Please
Not Again!...................................... 42

Chapter 7: God's Hands 55

Eternity 67

1

Married to a Monster

You know the old saying "If God takes you to it, he will take you through it"? I can testify to this because he brought me through the most tragic seasons of my life, and I survived. I am living proof that God keeps his promises.

My favorite Bible verse is Jeremiah 29:11 which states, "For I know the plans I have for you declares the Lord, plans to prosper you and not to harm you, plans to give you a hope and a future." God's plan for my life turned out to be a lot different than my plan. He saw the bigger picture and patiently waited for me to stop being the prodigal daughter and come back home. He never gave up on me or left my side even, though I didn't always trust he knew what he was doing but he did. And for that I am eternally grateful.

My tragic season began in 1989 when I was in my midtwenties. I was not living my life like the Lord wanted me to live it. I knew better. My mom always had our family in church when we were growing up. We prayed at dinner and at bedtime. I was just young. I wasn't a bad person; but I was going to bars, dancing, and drinking with my friends. One night while at a bar in Dallas, I met a man. He asked me to dance, and I did. Later that evening, he kissed me and asked for my phone number. I am not sure why, but I gave it to him. I was not as attracted to him as I was to the idea of finding someone to start a life with. My friends and family were having babies and moving on with their lives. I wanted to do the same.

Four months later, he asked me to marry him. Against my better judgment, I said yes. Deep down inside of my soul, I knew it was not the right thing to do, but I did it anyways. My parents were not happy with my decision. They tried to talk me out of marrying him. They told me it was a mistake, and it would never last. Instead of listening to my parents' wisdom, I went ahead with my plans. We were married on January 27, 1990.

A SEASON OF TRAGEDY

We had our honeymoon in beautiful San Antonio, Texas. One of Texas's most romantic cities. This is the night I saw the real man that I had married. I realized I had made a grave mistake and married a monster. I saw nothing in the four months we dated that would lead me to believe he was this way. His behavior that night was a total shock to me, and I didn't know what to do about it.

The first night of our honeymoon, I started my menstrual cycle. This infuriated him. He blew up and slammed his fist against the wall and accused me of somehow making this happen on purpose. I was appalled at his behavior. What? I was caught off guard with such real anger he was demonstrating about something I had no control over. He was intense and animated to the point I thought he might become violent. Was he really that naïve about women and how menstruation works? We had a huge fight yelling and screaming at each other. I was afraid. Nothing made sense. Eventually, he calmed down and apologized but not before I saw the monster I had just married. What else could I do but accept his apology.

In our family, husbands and wives worked things out. We did not just call it a day and get a divorce. I felt trapped and scared from the first night. What or who did I marry? My mom and dad's marriage was by no means perfect. They had their share of struggles and fights. I knew that married life would have its moments. I was fully aware there would be ups and downs. However, my parents always made up. They were married for over forty years.

From the beginning, my marriage was volatile. We would fight about everything. There was no time in my marriage where he was ever sweet or loving. The evil started from the honeymoon and lasted six long miserable years. The verbal and physical abuse was a constant thing.

I was never allowed to leave the house without him. His jealousy left me trapped without a life of my own. If I said hello to the Walmart greeter, I was accused of being adulterous. He would throw fits of rage if he didn't get his way. It was normal for him to threaten to take his own life if he didn't get what he wanted. When he was angry, he would get in my face and headbutt me so hard it would knock me off balance.

So you can imagine the emotional roller coaster in my heart when I found out four weeks into the marriage that I was pregnant. Oh, dear God, what have I done? Now it's not just me. I'm bringing a baby into this situation. Having my first child was supposed to be the best time in my life. I didn't want to bring a baby into this hell I was living in. I did not know what to do. I could not tell my parents and admit they were right. My dad would have spent the rest of his life in prison if I told him my husband was abusive. I could not live with that. This was my mistake, and no one else needed to suffer for it. But now I was bringing a baby into this hell. God help me; God forgive me.

Nine months later, I was blessed with a beautiful baby boy. I named him Aaron. I had loved before, but this love was different. The first time I held him, I knew what true love was. I thanked God every day for this wonderful gift.

When Sam held Aaron, I prayed it would change him. I wanted him to feel true love when he looked into Aaron's eyes. I hoped it would make him a loving dad. He received no such blessing. He was jealous from the moment Aaron was born. He simply could not handle seeing me give so much attention to our son. As Aaron grew, so did his jealousy. He thought it was funny to teach Aaron to say bad words. Not the small curse words but the graphic ones. When we fought, he would use the foul language of the devil no matter if Aaron was in the room.

He could not hold a job to provide for his family. He had twenty-six jobs in six years. He would sit on the couch and play video games while I worked, cleaned the house, and took care of Aaron. I made just enough money for rent and day care. Sam was a very selfish person. He put himself before everything and everyone. To get what he wanted, he would lie with no remorse. He let me know early on in our marriage that what he said and did when he left the apartment was none of my business.

Before I met Sam, I had excellent credit. Companies would send me unsolicited credit cards in the mail, even at my young age. It took him no time to ruin my credit. If he saw something he wanted, he just bought it. He never cared if there was money in the bank to cover it. This caused our checks to bounce, and with that, there were fees. As you can imagine, our budget was very tight with me being the only one working. He would run up the long-distance phone bill. He maxed out the credit cards I had before I married him. It was my credit he was destroying. When not having money got in his way, his parents would bail us out. The only

A SEASON OF TRAGEDY

thing he cared about was having electricity so he could play his video games.

Divorce never crossed my mind back then, but I do look back and think I should have done it. I was so young, and things are not like they are today. Divorce is commonplace. I had seven aunts on my mother's side. They all had rocky marriages, and none of them got a divorce. At this point, divorce was not an option. I had made my bed, and now I had to lie in it. Romans 7:2 states, "By law a married women is bound to her husband as long as he is alive." I felt like God would be disappointed in me if I left him.

Sam was not only a narcissist and selfish, but he was also very shallow. He accused me of stealing his parents from him. One year for Christmas his parents gave me a watch and a nice outfit. They gave him a brand-new car. After leaving his parents' house, we got into a huge fight. He said, "They love you more than me because you got two presents, and I only got one."

We were fighting so loudly Aaron began to cry in the back seat. I told him, "Pull over, and just let me out of the car."

I went to get Aaron out of his car seat to console him, and he said, "You are not leaving me." He got out of the car. I told him I was tired of everything, and I didn't want to live like this anymore. He slammed his fist through the back glass of his brand-new car, shattering the glass all over Aaron. Again, he said, "You are not leaving me."

I was so upset with him for scaring Aaron and shattering glass all over him. I told him to take me back to his parents' house. I wanted him to tell his parents what he had done. Someone needed to see what he was capable of. I thought, for sure, his parents would be concerned and be on my side because of what happened to their grandson. No such luck. His mom made excuses for him. She said that when he gets mad, he just can't help himself. I don't know why I didn't leave him right then and there, but I continued to stay.

One Saturday morning, I woke up smiling. He asked me what I was smiling about, so I told him. I said I had a wonderful dream last night. I told him, "I dreamed I killed you and got away with it." The dream did not come true, but I did get the bed to myself for three nights. He slept on the couch. I had a moment of weakness in my thoughts. I do regret it, and I have made peace with God.

Sam was very mean to Aaron. One time, he slapped Aaron in the face and left his handprint on his cheek. He was mad because he would not stop crying. I told him I would kill him if he ever laid a hand on my child again. He would always apologize and say he didn't mean too. I took Aaron to day care the next day, and they questioned me about the bruise. I explained my husband had a temper, and he got mad at Aaron because he was crying. The day care worker said she would report it to Child Protective Services if they ever saw bruises on him again. I don't understand why I didn't leave him. I guess I was too proudful to admit that everyone was right about him.

2

The Beginning of the End

The toxic environment never ended. I worked for a computer company as an administrative assistant. The owners were condescending and yelled at the employees. Maybe it was my imagination, but I felt they didn't think highly of women. I was tired from the stress of my home life, and now I was struggling at my job. It felt like I had three jobs: I worked a full-time job, I was a mom, and I fought with the monster. From the time I woke up until the time I went to sleep at night, I had no relief from the hard life I was living.

Meanwhile, Sam would leave the house in the morning, telling me he was going to look for a job. He would wait for me to leave for work, then he would go back home and play video games. One day, I left work early because I was not feeling well. When I got home, he was there on the couch playing his game. I went crazy with anger. I was done. I quit. I was so tired of the lies. I was going to finally leave him and that horrible job. I went to work the next day and typed my letter of resignation and tried to give it to my boss. He was heading out the door to a meeting and told me to put it on his desk. I was very frustrated because I wanted to give it to him in person. I put the letter in my desk drawer and went home. I would know in a few days it was God watching out for me. Over the weekend, I found out I was pregnant again. Unfortunately, I was still trapped in this horrible marriage and stressful job. There was no way I could walk away from the medical insurance.

Turns out, I needed the insurance for more than the birth of my baby boy Nicholas. He would spend the first three months of his life in the hospital. He was born with a condition called choanal stenosis and was transported to the Children's Medical Center in Dallas. The pathway from behind his nose to his airway was clogged, making breathing difficult. Nicholas had the best ear, nose, and throat doctor in Dallas to take care of him. But he was not able to do the surgery because he didn't have small-enough instruments. Nicholas was a tiny baby and only weighed 5.2 ounces when he was born. The doctor wanted us to wait until Nicholas got older, then he would do surgery to correct his nose. I was terrified. I prayed and prayed for a blessing. When we went back two months later, the pathway was clear, leaving the doctor perplexed with no explanation. I told him that I knew why it was gone. I knew God had heard my prayers, and he healed Nicholas's nose.

During the time Nicholas was in the hospital, I didn't work. I stayed at the hospital with him. We had to move in with Sam's parents because we couldn't make ends meet. The breadwinner was with her son at the hospital, and the monster was not working.

Him being unemployed got us deeper and deeper in debt. I could not take it anymore. I was fed up with him and told him to get a job by Friday or else. He asked me what does "or else" mean. I told him if he was not employed by Friday, I would move back to Henderson to be with my family. So he quickly found a job. The company wanted to send him to Mexico for training. His mother absolutely forbid him from going to Mexico. We had

A SEASON OF TRAGEDY

a huge fight, and I made him choose between his mother or his family. I was surprised he stepped up and went to Mexico to train for six weeks. When he returned, he started working, and we were able to save enough money to move out of his parents' house. Not long after we moved out, he quit this job, and we were once again behind on our bills, including rent. I had to return to work to support the family. Both the boys went to day care, and it was expensive. My salary paid the rent and day care. We lived on what little money was left. I was on him constantly to find and keep a job. I would leave for work, and he would be home playing video games. He would lie to me and tell me he had good prospects and would have a job soon.

Sam got a job when Nicholas was about eleven months old. It was just down the street from our apartment. He had been there for a few weeks, and I was excited to have the extra money. Finally, a little relief.

About a month into this new job, I received a call from my sister telling me her ex-husband had been killed in a car wreck. This was horrible news. My sister still loved her ex-husband. I still loved my brother-in-law. My heart was so sad for her two sons, my nephews. I thought about the boys not having a father. He was a great dad. She asked me to come and be with her. Without hesitation, we were on our way.

To give my sister some time to heal and process what had happened, I brought my nephews home with me. I took a few more days off from work and spent time with them. We went to the zoo, the park, and had a great time. Sam was jealous because he wanted to go with us, but his job would not let him take off.

The next day, he came home from work early. I asked him if he got fired again. He said no. He explained the company was doing inspection, and he was told to go home until Monday. He said they were going to pay for the time the employees were off work. This sounded fishy to me, and I knew he was lying. He spent the next few days going places with my nephews, the boys, and me. The whole time he was not working, I felt I was being deceived. No surprise I was!

After my nephews went home, I went back to work. I received a phone call from Sam's boss. He was really confused as to why I was at work and not at the funeral. When I asked what funeral, he said your son's funeral. I asked him what he was talking about. He said Sam had told him Nicholas was in

A SEASON OF TRAGEDY

the hospital and had passed away. The monster showed him photos of Nicholas that were taken when he was a baby at Childre's Medical Center. He told his boss the funeral was in east Texas. His boss told him to take a few days and let him know if there was anything he could do. His boss explained the reason he was calling. He said he tried to send flowers to the funeral home, but the address the monster gave him was to a car lot in Kilgore, Texas.

Sam's boss was so upset he told me to tell him not to come back to work because he was fired. I told him to watch the ten o'clock news. There would be a funeral—only, it was going to be Sam's funeral, not Nicholas. I could not believe my ears. Did I really hear him right? My mind was spinning; I began to cry. I was so upset my boss came to my desk to see what the matter was. I told her I was giving my two weeks' notice. After she heard what happened, she said, "Don't worry about the two weeks. Just get away from him."

I called my sister and told her what happened, and she said, "Well, what are you going to do about it." I told her to come and get me. I was leaving him and filing for divorce. I asked her to call Sam and tell him not to come home. I was extremely angry, and if I laid eyes on him, I would kill him. When she called him, he laughed and told my sister she won't kill me. He said he was going home.

She said, "Okay, go home, it's your funeral." She explained how angry I was with him. She told him I had asked her to raise my boys while I spent time in prison. She finally convinced him how serious I was. I know without a shadow of doubt I would have taken his life if he had come home. What he said about Nicholas was inexcusable. This is something only a monster would say about their own son. He wanted to say goodbye to the boys, so my sister took them to see him. I packed up everything except his belongings, and I left Dallas and moved in with my sister and her family.

I wanted to file for divorce right away but learned I had to live in Henderson for six months before I was able to file for divorce. Once the divorce was final, I felt free from him. No more violent fights, no more headbutts, no more bounced checks, no more verbal abuse, no more horrible home life, and no more worrying about whether he had a job or not. The boys still had to see him when he picked them up for his visitation. At first, he would come and get them for his weekends. He would tell the boys, "When Mommy cools off, we will move back to Dallas to be with me." After a while, he stopped coming to get them for his weekends. He would call and promise he would be there for every baseball game and every karate practice, but he never showed up.

He paid child support in the beginning, but that didn't last either. He would make a small payment occasionally, but he never paid what the court ordered him to pay. He kept getting more and more in arrears. When he talked to the boys, he told them he never missed a payment. One Sunday after picking the boys up from their visitation, Aaron asked me a question that startled me. He said, "Dad told me to ask you for the child support money. He said the money I pay your mom is yours and Nicholas's money, not hers." When we got home, I explained what child support was and told him his dad had not made a payment in over a year. Aaron was really upset with him for lying. He told me he never wanted to see him again.

One Saturday, Sam called and said he was in Henderson. He asked if he could see the boys. He said he was at the park and asked if I would bring them. I agreed, and when we got there, he introduced me to his new fiancé. I was so happy for him. I was glad he was getting married and moving on with his life. His fiancé's name was Stacy, and she seemed nice at the time. I would find out later this was far from the truth. She was verbally and physically abusive to my boys. One weekend, Aaron came home with a handprint on his thigh. You could tell it was a women's handprint because the outline of her fingernails left bruises. I called Sam and told him there would be consequences if I saw more bruises on either of my children. A few weeks after our visit to the park, I was at work, and I received a phone call from Stacy. She wanted to talk to me about Sam. I am not sure why she would ask me, but she asked if I thought it was a good idea for her to marry him. I gave her my true advice. I told her not to do it because one day she would wake up and find she was married to a monster. She thanked me for being honest with her. She did not listen to me and married him anyways. She endured the same toxic behavior from him and found herself with two children and him not working.

3

Life after the Monster

Aaron and Nicholas could not have been more different from each other. Aaron, my oldest, was loving and liked to cuddle. He had a sweet spirit about him. When the boys were little, they would say things that were so cute. It was dinnertime, and we were about to say the prayer. Aaron asked if he could say it, and I said, "Yes, you may." He was only about four years old. He stood up on his chair, turned around, put his head on the bar, and said "God, God, Gooodddd." He turned around and said, "Momma, he is not listening to me. He must be taking a nap." I laughed so hard tears were flowing down my face.

Nicholas, my youngest, informed me when he was seven years old, he no longer wanted to be called Nicholas. He wanted to be called Nick. He had a dry sense of humor, but when he said or did something, you were going to laugh. Nick gave what I liked to call drive-by hugs. He would put one arm around you, and that was it. I would grab him and give him a big bear hug. I would tell him I don't want a drive-by hug. I want a real hug. He would say, "Momma, I already gave you a hug." One time I took him to the doctor for a checkup; we were put into an exam room. Nick saw a stuffed bear on a shelf and asked me to get it down for him. He laid the bear on the exam table. He sat down in the doctor's chair and said to the bear, "What seems to be the problem with you today?" Suddenly, he jumped up rolling the doctor's chair out from underneath himself. He yelled at me, "Get the crash cart! We're losing him!" He started performing CPR on the bear with compressions to his chest and blowing breaths into his mouth. I started laughing so loud and hard the doctor came in to see what was going on. After the doctor left, I asked Nick where he learned about CPR, and he said at school.

A SEASON OF TRAGEDY

The boys and I lived the first year with my sister and her family. Then we moved in with my parents and lived with them for nearly two years. I was trying to save money to move out on my own. I didn't want to be a bother to anyone. I wanted to prove I could make it on my own. One day, my dad said to me, "It's time you remarried. I have someone I think would make you a great husband. Would you be willing to meet him? He works with me, and he is a good Christian man. He is divorced and has three older children."

His name was Andy, and they worked together at Pine Cove Christian Camps in Tyler. Little did I know, my dad talked to Andy and told him all about me. He told him, "She will make you a great wife." Andy had no intentions of getting married again but agreed to meet me. A few weeks later, Pine Cove was having their Christmas party. I went with my parents to meet Andy. He was tall, handsome, and had a mustache. Aaron would not be happy about his mustache. Aaron prayed one night for God to give his mommy a new husband, "But please, God, let him be a good Christian man, have a good job, and not have a mustache." I guess two out of three is not bad.

Seven months after our first date, we were married. We got married in July 1999. It was very hot that year, and our wedding reception was outdoors. We were not crazy, even though everyone thought we were. We both had been married before and didn't want to spend a lot of money on a wedding. We wanted something small and inexpensive. There was a church next door to my parents' house. We asked the preacher if we could be married in the church. The reception was in the backyard of my parents' house.

On two sawhorses laid two old wooden doors. Covering the entire top of the doors were the most beautiful red tomatoes. Andy grew more than we would have ever been able to eat that summer. He started giving away tomatoes as people would leave the reception. No one left the reception without a bag full of tomatoes. It made him happy to share in the fruits of his labor. He loved everything about gardening, especially the fact that I would help him gather the vegetables.

He started in January every year, planting onions and the other winter vegetables. Then in the spring, he would plant tomatoes, peppers, cabbage, cucumbers, and purple hull peas. He would try to grow something different each year. He loved the

A SEASON OF TRAGEDY

challenge of seeing if he could make them grow. If he was successful in making it grow, it would be added to the list every year after that. We would sit down in late December and create a list of what I wanted him to plant in the spring garden. Of course, my choice was always tomatoes, cucumbers, and purple hull peas.

He loved working in the dirt. That is what he did best. We always had a garden. Each year, it would get bigger and bigger. He would be in the garden every evening, watering and caring for his plants. One evening, he told me to come and watch what he was doing. I went and stood at the edge of the garden. He was watering the plants, and little birds were flying into the middle of the streams of water and opening their wings as if they were taking a bath. They would swoop down and get a drink of the water and then fly off again. Andy said it was one of the best feelings in the world to watch his plants grow. Knowing full well we would have more than enough vegetables to eat and some to give away to family and friends.

Andy and my boys bonded quickly. While we were dating and for a while after we married, they called him Mr. Andy. One day, Nick came running through the house, yelling, "Dad, Dad, where are you?" The boys called him dad from that point on. Aaron was all about the outdoors; Andy and Aaron bonded over hunting and fishing. Andy watched wrestling with Nick every Monday night. They called it He-Man Chili Night. They would eat chili and watch wrestling together.

After living in Henderson for a few years, Andy and I moved to Chandler and bought a house. It seemed our family had settled into the new house and life in Chandler. The yard was big enough for the boys to play baseball. They made friends in the neighborhood, and at times, there would be eight to ten boys in our yard playing ball. Andy would always say, "You're killing my grass." I would reassure him we could grow more grass, but the boys would only be young once.

Life was good, and the boys were glad to have someone in their lives that did things with them. Andy never missed a baseball game, ball practice, or anything important going on in their lives. He was there at night to tuck them into bed and say their prayers. Andy was good to me; he loved me, and I felt loved. He treated me like a princess and held my hand everywhere we went. Several of my friends told me, "Connie, you have a good man.

A SEASON OF TRAGEDY

Don't let him go." I had no intention of letting him go. I loved this man with all my heart.

We had tried several different churches in the community but finally decided on Faith Baptist Church of Chandler. It was not a very big church. The people seemed nice and were very friendly. We attended church services with the boys, and they got involved in the youth group with some of their friends from school.

I was happy, and everything seemed to be going well. I applied for a job at Pine Cove and got a job working in human resources. Every day, Andy would come to my office after getting off work and wait for me. We would follow each other home, which was only fifteen miles. The shorter distance was good for Andy. He had been working for Pine Cove for nearly eight years and driving back and forth from Henderson to Tyler before we moved to Chandler. This drive would take him more than an hour every evening. He said he didn't mind the long commute, but after being in Chandler for a few weeks, I could tell he enjoyed getting home in twenty minutes instead of an hour. He had more time to spend in his garden. Life was good. It was simple, and I was happy.

CONNIE CAPPS

In March of 2000, my mom called me at work and said she was taking my dad to the hospital. She said he was having chest pains, and she thought he might be having a heart attack. I told her I was on my way to the hospital. She said to wait until she knew more of what was going on. This was my dad! I didn't listen. I left work and drove straight to the hospital. When I arrived, he was in the cardiac unit and was making a fuss about all of us being there. He kept saying, "I am okay. I just have a little indigestion."

I had to go to the bathroom, so I stepped out of the room. As I left, I saw a doctor studying an X-ray. You could see a large mass in the middle of someone's chest. I remember thinking to myself that someone was about to get some really bad news. When I returned from the bathroom, the doctor was still looking at the X-ray. As soon as I passed him, he followed me into my dad's room. Instantly, my heart was in a million pieces. I started crying; my mom asked me what was wrong. I couldn't say anything. I knew it was my dad who was about to receive the bad news. We were all about to get the bad news. The doctor told us that there was a baseball-sized mass in the middle of his chest. He wanted to do some tests to see if the mass was malignant. My dad was diagnosed with lung cancer and was told it was inoperable. The tumor was growing in the aorta, which fed blood to the lungs.

My dad fought hard to beat the cancer. He did chemotherapy and radiation. Unfortunately, he lost the battle eight months later. While on his deathbed, he talked with Andy and me. He said he used to worry about the boys and me. He said, "I don't worry anymore since you married Andy." Then he said to Andy, "Take care of my girl and my two grandsons." Andy promised him he would, and he did. On October 29, my dad went home to be with his heavenly Father. It was a very hard time for me. My dad was such an important part of my life. He was the man I looked up to. I had a lot of respect for my dad.

4

Tragedy

One Sunday, January 1, 2006, I woke up a little after 9:00 a.m. and started doing housework. I was headed to the utility room to put on a load of clothes. The boys had been up for a while and were outside playing basketball. Suddenly, Aaron burst through the front door and said, "Momma, Grandpa Ray is here, and he is crying." I went to the door. My father-in-law looked at me with sadness in his eyes.

He said, "Connie, please sit down. I need to tell you something."

I asked him, "What is it? Has something happened?"

A SEASON OF TRAGEDY

He looked at me with as much compassion as he could and ask again, "Connie, please sit down."

He began to say something and then he stopped, a stream of tears came flooding down his face. He said, "I don't know how to tell you this. Andy was in a car wreck this morning."

I asked if he was okay. "Where is he? I need to go to him."

My father-in-law said, "No, he is not all right. His truck left the road and hit a tree, and he didn't make it." He went on to explain that the wreck happened at around 5:00 a.m. this morning.

I said, "No, he is in Henderson at the deer lease." I began to cry and scream, "No, NO, please, God, not Andy."

My father-in-law just wrapped his arms around me and hugged me tightly. His tears were coming even harder than before.

Aaron started screaming at his grandpa. "No, he is not dead. You are a liar. My dad is not dead. He can't be. He just can't be."

I jumped up and grabbed Aaron and gave him a big hug and said, "It's okay, Aaron, we are going to be okay."

He said, "What are we going to do without Dad?" I looked around the room, and my eyes found Nick. He had a small tear streaming down his face. Immediately, he stood up and ran to his bedroom and shut the door. I wanted to go after Nick to console him, but Aaron had my attention at that moment. He was weeping so hard we both fell to the floor. He kept saying repeatedly, "Not Dad, no, Momma, not Dad." I was so overwhelmed with emotions I didn't know what to do.

I asked my father-in-law how he knew about this before I did. He explained the highway patrol got the license plate number off Andy's truck. It was registered at our old house in Henderson. Two highway patrol officers had gone to make the notification; no one was home. My uncle Earl was attending church next door and saw the officers. He went to talk with them. The officers asked if Andy still lived at this address. My uncle said, "No. Andy's mother-in-law lives here now." The officers told my uncle that there had been a tragic accident. Knowing that I would need family with me, my uncle called my mom. She called my father-in-law and asked him to come to my house. She wanted someone to be with me if the officers tried to notify me.

My father in-law looked at me and said, "How about you and the boys go to the house with me."

A SEASON OF TRAGEDY

I told him, "I need to call people, and I need to get some clothes washed." My mind would not let me accept the truth. I just kept thinking Andy would walk through the door at any minute, and this would all be a bad dream.

The phone rang; it was my mom, and she said, "Connie, I am on my way." I was crying so hard I could barely breathe.

She said, "Baby, I'll be there in about an hour and a half."

I said, "Please hurry, I need you." I hung up the phone, and it rang again. This time, it was my sister; she said she was on her way and would be here in a few hours. I asked if she had contacted my brother. She said Mom had called them both. I was asking her why, and she just kept telling me, "I don't know, sister, but it's going to be okay."

The phone calls started going out, and family members started showing up. Before long, my house was full of people, asking me what they could do to help. My answer was for them to pray. I sat in Andy's recliner, watching everyone trying to do something to help. In times like this no one knows what to do or say. Everyone just started doing chores. Some were washing clothes, others were doing the dishes, and some were making phone calls. I just sat there numb, not knowing how or what to feel. I was in shock. I could not believe the man I loved was gone.

Barely believing it myself, I had to call Andy's three children and tell them what had happened. Katrina, the oldest girl, said they were on their way. Katrina and Jessie lived in McAllen near the border. It would take them eight to ten hours to get to Chandler. John was in college in San Antonio and said he would be there as soon as he could.

When my brother arrived at my house, he asked me what wrecking yard Andy's truck was taken. I gave him the information. He took his wife, and they went to see the truck. My sister-in-law said when James rounded the corner and saw the truck, he fell to his knees. He could not believe what he was seeing. The truck was completely burned and mangled. He told his wife there was no way anyone could have survived.

Later that night, as everyone slept, I was praying, and God told me, "I loaned him to you for a *season* of time." I was lying on the love seat in my living room, trying not to disturb the rest of my family that had now gathered at my house. They came from Dallas and Houston. They had learned of the news before I did and had started the long

A SEASON OF TRAGEDY

drive to my house. "I loaned him to you for a *season* of time." Why, Lord, please tell me why this is happening? I needed to know why. Again, "I loaned him to you for a *season* of time."

I was not able to sleep. My mind would not let me. I just kept thinking about Andy. This wonderful man I had given my heart to. We had made all these plans. We were going to grow old together. We would sit in our rocking chairs on the front porch and spoil our grandchildren. We would watch them in the garden picking vegetables. Andy would surely teach them how to grow anything they wanted. Grandpa would have He-Man Chili Night with the grandkids. Now this had all changed. The man that held my hand everywhere we went was gone. My life was forever changed.

5

The Funeral

The morning of the funeral, I could hear the boys in the bathroom. Aaron said to Nick, "Here, let me help you with your hair. You want to look good for Dad's funeral, don't you?" It was the sweetest moment the boys had had together in a long time. I was so proud of Aaron for helping his little brother. I was so overwhelmed with the love they were showing each other I began to cry.

The funeral was held at the church we were attending in Chandler. There were many people who came—both of our families, friends, and some coworkers from Pine Cove. I barely remember anything about the funeral. I was still numb. I don't think I accepted it yet. I had to be strong for my boys. I was thinking about my new life without Andy and where we should go from here. I wanted to sell the house and move, but Aaron and Nick both said they didn't want to move. So we continued to live in the house Andy and I had bought.

The wreck was investigated at the scene by a highway patrol officer, and Andy was found to be at fault. The officer was convinced Andy was traveling toward Tyler and not toward Henderson. I told her he was going hunting in Henderson where his deer lease was. The officer said they had a witness that saw the whole thing. The witness stated he saw Andy's truck traveling toward Tyler, and the other car was traveling toward Henderson. I can't see how the witness could have seen anything. The witness was down a boat ramp, it was completely dark, there were no lights around, and both vehicles were black. There were trees lining the road at the top of the boat ramp. He told the officer he had been fixing a broken wire in his trunk and heard the crash. This means he was paying attention to his wire in the trunk then heard the crash. He saw the immediate aftermath and nothing before.

The patrol officer called me and questioned me about where Andy was going and why he had a gun in his truck. I explained he was going hunting in Henderson at his deer lease. She said, "No, he was coming back to Tyler."

I said, "Are you 100 percent sure?" I explained to her he would not turn around without calling me and letting me know. She said she had a witness and would not change the report. She was convinced my husband was at fault. I was very upset. I tried to convince her, but she was adamant and was not about to change her mind. She was rude and arrogant and said she didn't like being questioned.

This is what really happened. It was New Year's Eve, and the young man had been out partying. He was coming home to where he lived in Tyler. He topped the hill doing 90 miles an hour and hit my husband head-on. When the vehicles hit, the impact was so great it broke the drive shaft in Andy's truck in half. It pierced the gas tank, causing Andy's truck to explode.

The young man's car also caught fire. We found out later in the investigation that he had been drinking and had cocaine, Versed, and a lot of other drugs in his system. The young man survived the wreck but spent months in the hospital. His burns were so extensive he was burned over 80 percent of his body. His parents were so afraid I was going to sue they hired a lawyer the next morning.

A SEASON OF TRAGEDY

For a year and a half, I tried to get the police record changed. I didn't want the report to say Andy was at fault. DPS was convinced Andy was traveling toward Tyler and not toward Henderson. My insurance company hired a professional reenactment team from Houston. When they concluded their investigation, they found Andy was traveling toward Henderson like I had always said. The young man's insurance company did their own investigation and agreed with my insurance company's findings. Even with both insurance companies agreeing on who was at fault, DPS still would not change the report.

The very last time I went to the DPS office, I wanted to talk face-to-face with the investigating officer who worked Andy's wreck and ask her why she would not change the report. Especially since both insurance investigators show he was not at fault. Her boss stated she was on assignment out of town. The lieutenant said that once an officer makes up their mind, they will not change it.

My father-in-law was with me; he asked the lieutenant if he could *100 percent* prove that Andy was at fault and traveling toward Tyler. He looked at the both of us and said, "No, I cannot." The report was never changed, but they finally admitted they could not prove which direction my husband was going. I looked at the lieutenant and said, "I will not be back because I got what I wanted. I know my husband was not at fault."

I did not understand how Andy's life could be cut so short when we had so many plans. The day before his accident, the boys and I had gone to Andy's parents' house for a Christmas party. Andy went hunting that morning and said he would meet us there around lunch.

When he arrived, I was upset with him. He took me outside and asked what was wrong. I said to him, "When you left this morning, you forgot to tell me goodbye."

He said, "No, I didn't. I told you goodbye and gave you a kiss." He grabbed my hands and said to me, "Mrs. Tate, if the Lord is willing to let me live another fifty years, I want to spend all that time with you." The next morning, he was killed.

I wanted to see the photos of the accident. My family tried to convince me that I would not be able to handle seeing the photos, and it might give me nightmares. I was not able to see or physically touch his body and say goodbye. I needed something concrete to prove he was really gone. My heart knew it, but my mind wanted proof. Even if it meant I had to see the photos. A few days later, I called the camera shop and told them I wanted a copy of the pictures. They asked me several times, "Are you sure?" The day I picked them up, I could not wait until I got home. I immediately opened the envelope. As I looked at each photo, my mind had its proof. It was Andy's truck, and now it was real. As the tears fell, I kept asking God why. It was a gruesome and disturbing sight, but I was glad I insisted on seeing them. In a weird way, it gave me some closure.

Nothing could ease the pain I was feeling, but Andy found a way from the grave to take care of me. He had life insurance. It was such a gift from him. I didn't have to worry about money on top of my grief.

I decided to take the boys on a vacation. I thought the change of scenery would do us some good. I took the boys to Playa del Carmen in Mexico. I asked my mom to join us because I didn't want to go by myself. She knew I needed to get away, and she was excited to go. She had never been that far out of the country. Neither of my boys had ever flown before. We had a great time, but when we came home, the reality of Andy being gone was still there.

School was about to start for the boys, and it was time to buy school clothes. In the past, I was not able to afford expensive clothes for them. This year was going to be different. I had money to buy them the clothes they really wanted.

We were in Old Navy shopping. I asked Aaron if he liked the jeans I was holding. He said, "Yes, Momma," but I could tell it wasn't what he really wanted.

I looked at him and said, "If you could have any jeans, which ones would you choose?"

He said, "I would really love American Eagle jeans."

I looked at him and said, "Let's go to American Eagle."

Aaron kept saying, "No, their jeans are too expensive."

I looked at him and said, "Baby, don't you worry about the money. I want you to have whatever you want."

A big smile came across his face, and he said, "Are you sure?"

I said yes.

He picked out several pairs of jeans and some shirts. He was smiling from ear to ear. I asked Nick if he wanted any American Eagle jeans.

A SEASON OF TRAGEDY

He looked at me and said, "I don't care about my clothes. I just want a pair of Michael Jordan tennis shoes."

I said, "Where do we get them?"

He said, "At Foot Locker."

That was so much fun to see the smiles on their faces, being able to get the clothes and shoes they never had before. I know I spoiled them, but at the time, it was something that made both of us happy. The boys and I lived in the house for two more years.

6

Not Again, God, Please Not Again!

The preteen years were hard. The boys started arguing and fighting a lot. They didn't have the same interests and could not agree on anything. Nick was really into sports, and Aaron was into girls. He started talking about girls all the time.

For the first year after Andy died, my mother lived with the boys and me. It was nice having her there when the boys got home from school. She would make sure they were doing their homework before they went outside to play. I had gone back to work at Pine Cove. It was too much for me. I missed Andy so much. Being there just brought up too many memories. I decided I needed a change.

A SEASON OF TRAGEDY

I wanted something different, something I had never done before. I decided to become a massage therapist.

Aaron and Nick grieved so differently; Aaron was very verbal while Nick held it all in. I started them in counseling. The grief counselor's name was Elwood Stetson. Sounds like a movie star. He was a great man of God and worked with the boys on their grief. Aaron saw Mr. Stetson more than Nick. He took Andy's death very hard. Nick didn't show much emotion and said he was all right.

Aaron's anger was very much a part of our lives. He would get so mad and throw fits of rage when he got the least bit upset. One day, Aaron got mad at Nick and started beating on him. I called 911, and they sent a sheriff's officer out. He had a long talk with Aaron and told him he could not put his hands on his brother. Aaron was polite and told him he would not do it again. The officer said to him, "If I get called back out here, I will be taking you away in handcuffs."

For a few weeks after this incident, it seemed like Aaron and Nick were getting along. They had lots of friends that loved to come to our house. We always had more than one or two of their friends spending the night. Aaron's friends were Jeremy and Mitchel. Both boys were so sweet and kind. They loved to spend the night because I would get up and fix them huge pancakes.

Nick's best friend was a boy named Kevin. He was the sweetest young man who told me he wanted to come and live with us. He said his grandmother would not mind. I told him he was able to come over anytime, but he could not live with us because I didn't want to take him from his grandmother who loved and was raising him.

One night, I was in my bedroom, and I heard Nick scream, "Momma, he is hitting me!" I went down the hall, and there was Aaron hitting Nick with a wire clothes hanger. He was yelling at Nick as Nick was trying to hide behind a dresser. I told Aaron to stop, and he ignored me. I tried to take the hanger away, and he yanked it back. I told him if he didn't stop, I would call 911.

He looked at me and said, "Good, call them. I know you love Nick more than you love me." I called 911, and the same sheriff's officer came back to our house. When he walked in, Aaron was calm and was sitting on the couch. The officer asked me what had happened. I explained the situation, and he turned and looked at Aaron.

A SEASON OF TRAGEDY

He said, "Young man, what did I tell you would happen if I got called back out here?"

Aaron looked at me and said, "No, Momma, don't let him take me."

My eyes were filled with tears. I didn't want him to take Aaron, but I didn't want the fighting to continue. I looked at Aaron and said, "Baby, you can't keep hurting your brother. I don't love him more than I love you. I just can't have you getting mad and someday really hurting him."

The officer told Aaron to stand up, and he did. He told him to turn around, and he placed the handcuffs on him. He started to lead him out the door, and Aaron said, "Momma, please don't let him take me." I was crying so hard. I told the officer I didn't want him to go.

He said, "I am sorry. There was a physical altercation, and I told him what would happen if I got called back out here."

I asked him where he was taking him, and he said to juvenile detention. I asked when he would be coming home, and he said that would be up to the judge. He said for me to contact the juvenile detention center in the morning, and they would let me know when he would be going before the judge.

Of all the hard things in my life, that moment didn't compare to the pain I was feeling seeing my baby being put into the back of a sheriff's car and driven away. I stood there on the porch for a long time, crying. Nick came out and said, "Momma, come in. It's going to be okay." He looked at me with tears in his eyes and said, "I didn't mean to get Aaron arrested. I should have just let him beat me up."

I told him, "No, it was not your fault. Aaron needs help with his anger, and I was going to get it for him."

Aaron saw the judge, and she put him on probation for six months. She told him she didn't want to see him in her court ever again. Aaron was released after spending three days in juvenile detention. He came home, and we sat down to talk. I told him I missed him so much.

He said, "Momma I am glad you called 911. Spending time in there has really been an eye-opener. I know what I did was wrong, and I should have been punished for beating up my little brother." He gave Nick a hug and apologized to him. From that moment on, the relationship between the two of them changed. They still argued occasionally, but there was no more fighting.

A SEASON OF TRAGEDY

Aaron turned fifteen, so I started to teach him driver's education. He seemed to really like to drive and wanted to drive everywhere we went. One day, he asked me if we could start looking at trucks for him. I said yes, and we found him a truck that I thought would be a good first vehicle for him. He found a job working at Brookshire Brothers sacking groceries. His job schedule didn't fit with my schedule, so we applied for him to get his hardship license so that he could go to work and school.

He was growing up and taking on a lot of responsibilities. Working part-time, going to school, playing football, and keeping a straight-A average. The first time he got his paycheck, he brought it to me and said, "Momma, what do I do with this money?"

I looked at him and said, "It's not my money. Do what you want."

He looked at me and said, "Are you serious? I don't have to give it to you."

I said, "No, it's yours to spend. You earned it." He was so excited he wanted to spend it right away. I feel like Aaron getting a job made him grow up a little.

On October 13, 2006, I was at work, and I received a phone call from the judge in Chandler where we lived. She was the same judge that had put Aaron on probation. She asked if Connie Tate was there. I said, "I am Connie," and she immediately asked to speak with my supervisor. I thought that was weird for her to ask for me but then ask for my supervisor. I transferred the call to my supervisor and went on about my work; about ten minutes later, Rob, my supervisor, came to my desk.

He said, "Connie, get your cell phone and come with me."

I asked him, "Why, and what is going on?"

He didn't answer me. He said, "Get your cell phone and come with me." He led me down the hall to his boss Joel's office.

Joel told me to come in and sit down. I was worried. I thought I was in trouble, but as I entered the room, I noticed there were a lot of other people in Joel's office. Two nuns and a few other people I didn't know. I asked him what was going on and he said, "Please sit down."

I looked at Joel and asked again, "What is going on?"

He said, "Connie, I need you to sit down."

I sat down, and my heart started pounding so hard, and I kept asking him, "What is going on?"

A SEASON OF TRAGEDY

Joel began to cry and said, "I don't know how to tell you this."

Connie, your boys were in an accident this morning on their way to school.

I immediately asked if they were okay. "Where are they? I need to get to them."

Joel said, "No, you can't."

I asked why, and he said, "They were killed." I began to scream at the top of my lungs, "No, GOD, NOT AGAIN! Please, God, not my boys. Please, God, not my boys."

Joel asked me for my cell phone; he wanted to know who I wanted him to call. I told him my mother. Joel asked me my mother's name, and I told him it was under "Mom" in my contacts. Joel left the room and told Rob, "Whatever you do, don't let her leave this room."

The nuns and the other ladies left. I looked at Rob and said, "Why my boys?"

He grabbed me and gave me a hug and said, "I don't know the answer to that question." He kept saying, "I'm so sorry, Connie, I'm so sorry." I told him I need to go I need to get to my boys. Rob said, "You can't. You must stay here with me."

I said, "No, I need to get to my boys. Let me go."

And he said, "Connie, I can't let you go."

I said to him, "Okay then, you have two choices. You either move out of my way, or I'm going to mow you down. I'm going to my boys."

He looked at me and said, "Okay," and he moved. I went out the back door, and there was Joel and the nuns. Joel was on the phone with my mom.

My mom asked Joel to put me on the phone. I said "Hello," and she said, "Baby, I'm on my way. I am in Houston and should be there in a few hours."

I asked, "Momma, why is this happening to me again?"

She said, "I don't know, but everything would be okay. I told her, "No, it will not be okay. My children are dead, and they will not let me go to them."

My mom said, "Connie, I will be there soon."

I looked up and my cousin Pam and my aunt Molly were there. Pam grabbed me and gave me a big hug. I remember weeping in her arms. My mom had called her sister Molly to come to the hospital to be with me until she could get there.

My mom kept saying it was going to be okay. I turned to Joel and said, "Where are my boys? What funeral home did they take them to? I need to go to them."

A SEASON OF TRAGEDY

Joel said, "Connie, you can't go to the funeral home."

I asked, "Why not?"

And he said, "Because the truck caught fire."

I am immediately passed out I went straight to the ground. When I woke up, all I could say was I wanted to die. "God, please let me come be with them."

My coworker Kathy was there, and she asked if there was anything she could do. Joel told her to call my doctor and get me some Xanax. He told her she is going to need it. Joel sent someone to pick it up at the pharmacy, and they began giving it to me. I asked Kathy to take me home. When I arrived home, I sat down in the living room in shock and numb. My aunt Molly and Pam stayed with me until my mom got there.

My mom had called my brother and told him what happened. He said, "I am on my way. When he arrived with his wife and children, they all gave me a big hug. My brother James asked what he could do to help. My sister-in-law Rose began directing people who were bringing food and answering phone calls."

My mom finally arrived, and as she held me, she said it was going to be okay. "Connie, God's got everything under control."

And I remember telling her, "Mama, I can't do this again. I've already been through it once," and she said, "Yes, you can. God will get you through this." My mom said my sister was in Cozumel and could not get back until Friday. She wanted to know if the funeral could be held on Friday. The boy's bodies were sent to Dallas for an autopsy. The police wanted to make sure there were no drugs or alcohol involved in causing the wreck.

The next morning, my brother took me to the funeral home to begin the funeral preparations. The funeral director said it was time to pick out the caskets. My brother helped me up and into the casket room. As soon as I walked in, I saw two white caskets. I said, "I will take these two." I turned around and headed back to my seat.

My brother said, "Wait, Connie, don't you want to look at any others."

I said, "No, I will take those two."

He said, "They have pink on the inside."

I said to the funeral director, "Can you change it to blue?"

A SEASON OF TRAGEDY

And he said yes. We finished with the arrangements, and I asked my brother to take me home.

The funeral was held at the gymnasium at Pine Cove. I asked the pastor Chris Legg if he would officiate the funeral. After Andy died, I prayed for God to help me find some godly men to help me with the boys. I knew they needed a godly presence in their lives now more than ever. Especially since their real father was not in their lives anymore.

God put it on my heart to ask two young men who worked at Pine Cove to be big brothers to Aaron and Nick. I asked Robbie Main and Mark Garcia if they would be interested. They both told me they would pray about it and let me know. A few days later, both contacted me and said they would be honored to do it. Once a week, Robbie and Mark would come to the house and get the boys and do something with them. They would take them out to eat, play basketball, or go to a movie.

Robbie was a big brother to Aaron; he thought the world of Robbie. Mark and Nick had a lot in common, they both loved sports and always had some game to talk about. The boys really loved the time they got to spend with them. Robbie and Mark made a big impact on the boys' lives. So much so I asked them both to deliver the eulogy at the funeral.

I don't remember much about the funeral, but I do remember Robbie and Mark speaking about the boys. Robbie told stories about his time with Aaron. Mark talked about Nick and how much Nick loved sports. There were over seven hundred people at the boy's funeral. My family and friends, almost the whole Brownsboro school, and the members of Pine Cove were in attendance.

7

God's Hands

After the funeral was over, I didn't want to be alone, so I asked my nephew Daniel to move in with me. My mother had remarried and was not able to move in. Without hesitation, Daniel said yes. He said he would have to go back to Houston to get his belongings and give notice to his job. A few weeks later, he moved in. He gave up his job and all his friends to be there for me. At first, I didn't want him to work. I wanted him to stay home and be there when I came home from work so I would not have to come home to an empty house.

My boss Rob was really outgoing and had a lot of friends. We talked about Daniel being new in town, so Rob invited him to hang out. Daniel quickly made friends and settled into his new life in Tyler.

Daniel was there for me when I was sad or down. He would hold me when I was crying. He didn't have to say anything, just having him there meant the world to me. We did everything together, going to the movies, going shopping—whatever I wanted to do he was right there with me.

After a year passed, Daniel and I agreed it was time for him to get a job. I think he was ready after being at home alone for all those months. He interviewed with a few companies, but God already had a plan in place. One of Rob's friends was a girl named Jana. She and Daniel had met when he started hanging out with Rob and his friends.

Jana was at home sick one day, and Daniel went to visit her. He bought some flowers and spent several hours visiting with her. They had a lot in common and became best friends right away.

Jana worked for her parents at CR Scrubs, and they hired Daniel for sales. He finally had a job and was able to see his best friend every day.

Jana and Daniel bought a house together and live in Gladewater. They had a beautiful baby boy and named him after my boys. Daniel always wanted to have a son named Declan. When Declan

A SEASON OF TRAGEDY

was born, Jana and Daniel gave him my boys' names as well. His name is Declan Aaron Nicholas Rast. It is mouthful to say, but he knows his name and why he was named after my boys. Jana and Daniel will never know how much this meant to me. To know my boys' names will continue and not be forgotten living through Declan.

For the next few years after the boys died, I would wake up every morning mad. I would be angry that I was still alive and left on this Earth. I would ask God, "Why? Why did you leave me here? Why didn't you let me go with the boys? I would be in heaven with you and my boys." God would remind me of my favorite scripture: Jeremiah 29:11.

He had a plan for my life. I just could not see it because I was trapped in my grief. My grief was a daily battle. I would cry, scream, weep, beg, and pray. I wanted answers. I wanted to know why. Why, Lord, did you allow this to happen?

On December 31, 2010, I was coming back to Tyler from visiting a friend. I was driving home on Interstate 20. My mind was not thinking correctly. I thought about ending my life. I told myself to speed up and get to 120 miles per hour and run off the road, and your problems will be all over. I started speeding up, and then God intervened. I started crying and pulled over to the side of the road. I began weeping and telling God I didn't want to live like this anymore. I was tired of wishing I was dead. I told the Lord my thought process had to change. I drove home, and the next morning, I woke up and was not mad. I began to think about my future. I wanted to make some changes, so I set some goals for my life in 2011. I told myself I was going to learn Spanish, pay off my bills, and get a boyfriend. Not exactly in that order, but that was "my plan."

Earlier in December, I was on Facebook and saw a message from someone in my past. It was Richard Capps; we had dated for a while after I graduated from high school. I answered the message, and we exchanged phone numbers. We called and spoke with each other every day. He told me about his life since high school, and I told him about mine. One night while we were talking, I told him about my goals for 2011.

When I told him I was going to get a boyfriend, he immediately stated it would not be him; he was never getting married again. A few weeks went by, and on January 24, I told him he was my boyfriend.

A SEASON OF TRAGEDY

He said, "Don't I get a say in the matter?"

I told him, "No, you are my boyfriend." I lived in Tyler, and he lived in Lufkin, but we seemed to make the long-distance relationship work for a year and half.

One weekend, I was visiting Richard, and he looked at me and said, "I think it is time you moved down here." I told him I was ready, but I would have to find a good job.

Again, God had his hand on my life. He gave me a great job working for people who were believers. My supervisor was Linda Daniel. Linda is beautiful both inside and out. She and I quickly became friends and would lift and encourage one another. We prayed together and would talk about our lives and how God had always been there for both of us.

Linda and I worked together for five years. Then God moved Linda to another job. We still talk and see each other but not every day. We still pray and encourage one another. Linda is my best friend, and I thank God for her and our friendship. Linda and I agreed in prayer that Richard would marry me.

We dated for a while longer, and we were married in 2013. Life with Richard has been good. He makes me feel very safe. He takes care of me and is there when I need him. Richard and I have been married for ten years in June 2023. God has blessed our marriage and protected us.

As I look back over the past fourteen years since the boys' wreck happened. I can see God's hands on me the entire time. God's grace and mercy were new each morning.

As I was going through my season of tragedy, I could not wait for it to be over. Many times, people would say to me, "I don't know how you do it. How do you get out of bed each morning? Connie, you are so strong to make it through this."

I would and still tell anyone who says this to me, "I only made it because God carried me through it. No one, I mean no one in their humanly form can survive this much tragedy without God. I am living proof with God you can survive anything. Even the death of your entire family can be something God uses for his good."

Sometimes I feel like a man in the Bible named Job. This man was blameless and upright; he feared God and shunned evil. Job had everything taken away from him. His wife, his children, and his wealth. He was afflicted with painful sores from the soles of his feet to the crown of his head.

A SEASON OF TRAGEDY

Yet he would not curse God. He continued to trust God. God restored everything back to Job because of his faith. God has restored many things in my life just like he did for Job.

This past October 2023, my boys have been living with their heavenly father for fifteen years. It is very hard to think that much time has passed. It still feels like yesterday, and I still struggle with their death daily. *But* God *is so good*; his unfailing love is there with me every step I take. I know he loves me and cares about me because he shows me his grace, mercy, and love each day.

This was a tragic season in my life. I didn't write this book for any recognition. All the glory and honor goes to God. The sole purpose of this book is to let the world know Jesus loves you. He wants to be your savior. He wants you to live with him in heaven. With him, you don't have to face anything, not even death, alone.

The Bible tells us to go unto the world and tell everyone the good news. The good news is that Jesus came to Earth to die on a cross so our sins would be forgiven. Your sins, my sins, every person living on the face of this Earth sins. He came because he loves you, and he doesn't want anyone to perish but have life everlasting.

If you don't know Jesus as your personal savior, how are you making it through this crazy life? With everything going on in the world, I can't imagine facing a single day without Jesus. The evil one is running rampant in our land. He is seeking to devour anyone and everyone he can. The reason we are living in such horrible times is because the devil knows his time is coming to an end. He is trying to fill hell with as many souls as he can.

My prayer for us is to empty hell *and* fill heaven*!*
We do this by telling the lost the good news. Jesus is the good news.

If you don't know him, Jesus can be your personal savior. All you must do is ask him to come into your life, forgive you of your sins, and acknowledge you believe in him. Some people say I have done so many bad things, he doesn't want me, or I am not good enough. None of these things matter. He doesn't want us for what we have done or who we are. We are all broken people that God can use if we let him. All the bad things will be forgiven when you accept him as your savior. He wants us to be a part of his family because he loves us. The Bible tells us Jesus's death removed our sins as far as the east is from the west.

A SEASON OF TRAGEDY

"As far as the east is from the west, so far has he removed our sins from us" (Psalm 103:12).

I first fell in love with Jesus fifty years ago. I was eight and gave my heart to him one Sunday. The preacher gave the invitation. I told my mother I wanted to give my heart to God. Both of my parents went up to the altar with me. I still remember how proud they were when I accepted Jesus as my savior.

If you have read my book to this point, I would like to thank you from the bottom of my heart. God loves you and would love to be your savior if you have never accepted him.

Even if you have accepted him but have strayed away, he still wants you. If you feel a tug on your heart strings that is the Holy Spirit prompting, you to accept Jesus or the Holy Spirit saying come home my prodigal child.

Pray this prayer with me:

> Dear Jesus, I acknowledge you are real, and you came to Earth to die on a cross for my sins. I ask you to come into my life and be my savior and forgive me of all my sins. Live in my heart and

> be the Lord of my life. In your precious holy name, "Jesus." Amen.

If you are a prodigal child and need to come home, he is waiting for you to call his name. Ask for his forgiveness, and he will give it to you. Do not let condemnation stop you from coming back to the feet of Jesus. He loves you and wants you home no matter what you have done.

> Dear Jesus, I repent of all my sins and ask for your forgiveness. I am sorry I have strayed away from you. I want to come home and be a part of the family of God again. Please welcome me back with open arms. Let your grace and mercy flow over me. In your precious holy name, "Jesus." Amen.

If you prayed either of these prayers, please share the good news with someone. Let them know you accepted Jesus as your savior. Or that you are

A SEASON OF TRAGEDY

no longer a prodigal. The God of the universe calls us his sons or daughters.

It is better to believe in him and find out he is real, than not to believe in him and find out he is real. You decide which way you believe and where you will spend eternity! Heaven or hell!

Eternity

Who's going with me!
If you know you have been *born again* and know that you know you are going to heaven, then *you* will be going with me. I can't wait to live with you in heaven for all eternity!

About the Author

Connie Capps is a first-time author of *A Season of Tragedy*, a book about a time in her life when she faced unthinkable life-changing events that forever changed her world. She was born in Houston, Texas, and then moved to the east Texas area before starting kindergarten. She was extremely shy as a child. Being the middle child of three with an older sister and a younger brother, she was often told she suffered from "middle child syndrome," always feeling caught in the middle.

Connie's mom and dad were middle-class people who taught their children about God, truth, love, and integrity. Their parenting style was traditional, but her dad always found a way to make the children learn from their mistakes. One time, Connie slammed the back door when going out to play. Her dad called her back in the house and made her open and close the door one hundred times.

This was not a simple open and close. She had to open the door and step outside, close the door and then open it again, and step back inside. This counted as one. When she got to ninety-nine, she had a bit of an attitude, so her dad made her start all over. She learned to never slam a door again.

Connie graduated from Diboll High School in 1982. She began working when she was fifteen years old. During her junior and senior years, she went to school in the morning and then worked in the afternoon. She never went to college.

Ms. Capps shares her house with three dogs and her wonderful husband, Richard. They call Diboll, Texas, home.